A VIEW TO A DOOR

A Collection of Abstract Essays: A Book of Peace and Harmony

JANE SUMMERS

AuthorHouse™
1663 Liberty Drive
Bloomington, IN 47403
www.authorhouse.com
Phone: 833-262-8899

Durga Madiraju

This book is printed on acid-free paper.

ISBN: 978-1-6655-6085-6 (sc)
ISBN: 978-1-6655-6084-9 (e)

Library of Congress Control Number: 2022910039

Print information available on the last page.

Published by AuthorHouse 06/06/2022

authorHOUSE®

https://www.summersmarketplace.com

CONTENTS

Acknowledgements

This book is dedicated to my father Dr. Chinta Chidananda Rao (Chief Medical Officer, South Central Railway), my mother Chinta Visalakshi, my husband Srinivas Madiraju, my daughter Anika Madiraju, my family and friends.

My sincere appreciation to all my friends, and well-wishers who have helped me at all times.

A View to a Door, is a 25-chapter book of abstract disquisition essays, and shows the different ways a construct can be related to a topic for a view of a door. This book is targeted to readers for a value of peace and harmony in different settings and can also be used as a reference to write abstract essays.

A View to a Door, is a Collector's Edition of abstract disquisitions, and contains chapters of essays that will help gather and relate different topics of essays for a new way of abstraction. It shows a view of different constructs that will help readers write their own abstract disquisitions –

Jane Summers

A view to a door
Abstract chapter 1

A view is a concept that explains what I can see and relate to my mind. A view can be used as a synonym to associate multiple words for a similarity or a dissimilarity of the meaning of the word.

An abstraction of the word view denotes a single word for a meaning of the word. A view for an abstract must be assembled using several synonyms for a word(s) to denote the meaning using similar synonyms through examples to create a picture in the mind of the user.

A view of several doors is a view of doors I see and relate in my mind. A view of a door can also be an association to a person, a group, an organization or others.

A view can be used to describe a profile, a characteristic, a feature for a view of a similarity, a dissimilarity, or others. A parallelism of a view to a door includes a poetry or prose, and is a grammatical match for structure, sound, and meter for the meaning of the word. Some examples of views include, a view of meadows that I can see for a view partial, meadows, a house with a fence for a view complete, and a view of several attributes of a home, meadows, and others that I can relate to my mind through a similarity or a dissimilarity to complement such a view for an association of the word to the construct.

A view for a door theory underlies an expression of a view seen several ways for an existing view of a door. A parallelism is a match for an expression, such as a view of meadows that I see for a complete view, meadows and a house with a fence for a view partial, and a view of several attributes of a home and meadows, and people I relate through a similarity or a dissimilarity to complement a view such as a barn, a park or others for a complete view from the perspective of a single mind.

A view must be related only for a congruity of something justified and agreed upon for a need or a situation such as a view for a value, view of education as a value, view of learning for a knowledge or improvement, view of a value generated through an innovation or invention for a purpose and use.

A view of a new meaning coined for an existing view can also include comparison perspectives such as a difference of a view of sky or earth. I do not need to fear that they do not meet but only that everything exists for peace and harmony. A view I describe a sky from an earth for a color, a texture, a pattern and others or for a quality such as a comfort, grace, appreciation and others is a view justified for a disquisition.

A view to a feeling - chapter 2

A State of Mind and A reason of a value

A view to a door of my feelings and emotions must be constrained for what I can control within my limit. Such a view of door can be constrained through use of variables for adjustment of a situation and a communication for a state of mind to translate for a value positive either for a gain or loss, even if the benefit is not in one's favor. A feeling is not just an outcome of effective models of instruction but must also serve as a means to account for and realize the method of teaching for a meaning and purpose of a subject to relate for a feeing (Reis & Roth, 2010).

A view of feelings are articles and are disquisitions of my views to a door of feelings for a period of time. A view for a disquisition can have several questions and answers. I need to choose the right question and answer for a door to open that can have a positive impact on my mind on others. A question of a view of a door for a state of mind must be associated and related to a view of a door for a question of a value of virtue and the answer communicated only for a value of a virtue positive. The answer should not be a detraction to the question.

A view of a door for a feeling of something dear or near such as a marriage or a birthday can be associated to fulfill a wish that is dear to me or others as long as it does not cause a negative impact on others. A view must include terms for restraint, containment for a boundary of the definition of a door of feeling and must unlock a door only for a value of a discussion, conversation, engagement or others for an outcome positive to renew a value of growth.

A view of a culture can be related for an extension, reservation, and for new additions and deletions for a positive outcome. This view can be applied to a family, a culture they belong to or to diverse cultures within and across countries and also for a culture of new undefined cultures.

A view of a door can also be for a tone or a mood for a setting, an appearance of a person in relation to a setting, a voice and a conversation. This view can be multiplied for new differences in a setting to provide new views of doors based on the above factors. Some examples of such views include learning of new languages for new knowledge, new way of conversing with others, an improved appearance and knowledge that helps promote a role in different areas of life.

A view can be for a view of a memory of several areas in life based on time and context for a setting for a value. Such a view of a recollection of a memory for a use and a path of progress makes a positive impact. Such views are based on values supported through a literature reference and must only be used to a path of value of progress to reconstruct values of knowledge for acquisition in engineering, business and other areas. In the personal area, a view of memory must be used to progress to a path of family values in education, nurturing of relationships and others.

A view of several theories can be constructed and analyzed based on literature review of new material supported and reconstructed for use in new or existing subjects. A relationship of a view for an abstraction of an association or a disassociation can be changed based on topics of positive values

A view of a door for a state of mind can also include a number of views that I can store in my mind. These memories are erased through time as new memories have a home for new thoughts and new values. A view of these doors must be eliminated through a transition to a state of mind for a new knowledge acquisition of education in different subjects for a failure in some area and others. A view of a such a door will open new doors of progress through a positive state of mind. A value of an education can be translated to a path of progress only through creating disquisitions for a use or a purpose, and communicating the disquisition as a subject of conversation for new knowledge acquisitions. These doors lead to path of progress in every area of life for a role of responsibility and match a role of subject matter expert for communication and delivery of a subject(s)

A view to a door of what I see changes every day and every season based on my interaction and conversation with family and others. A view for such a feeling of a door is embedded through these interactions translated through my mind. An example of a view of such a state of mind is, I know that I need to translate a state of mind always to a state of peace and harmony when encountering situations that require solutions in different areas of life.

A view for a state of mind of progress is translated when the values of education, are translated to a value of role undertaken for different purposes or subjects at different points of time and context for peace and harmony.

A view for a begin and an end - chapter 3

A disquisition for and of time

A view of a door can also be questioned for a begin and an end of a situation of a view to a door complete. The question of why a view exists, is related to several views of a door in my mind. Can the sunrise rise in the east and west, must be translated to a fact that a sunrise can only rise in the east. Some doors to a view have no answers and must be set to a different views to a door such as a sadness for a death to a happiness of another door for a view of a story of a situation complete.

A view for an exchange of a conversation can happen only when a life is true and exists. A conversation after can only be translated to a memory that I saved from my interactions with a person such as a message I recorded from an interaction, a conversation I remember, a festival I celebrated with a family and others in personal and social engagements. A view of a life of a father, mother, a daughter, son and others can be translated to a view to a door of my personal view of a door during a lifetime for a begin and an end I translated to book of memories.

A view for a begin and end of a leaf, a bud to a flower, a plant to a tree and a season for an end and others can be related and associated for a view of a grace, beauty of a season, and compared to other flowers and leaves of the same type and others for a new knowledge of a view to a door to create a new flower or leaf of different types for a view of a door of a begin and an end of a season.

Seasonal changes of views for a begin and end of a season can be also be translated for a dress of a color, a type of dress, a beauty for an art of a season. A life of a leaf that withered, a flower no more and a tree extinct are examples of differences for a begin and an end of a season.

A view of a door for a sound that begins and ends can be translated to a sound of breeze for a begin and end of a rain, a sound of quarrel or an altercation between people for a begin and end of a quarrel, a slight breeze of a petal or a flower curved during an afternoon or evening for a begin and end of the petal curve. The views to such doors can be remembered by writing them down in a notebook for use later as a begin and end of a view to a door for a begin and end of a situation.

A view of a door for a land not used for any purpose, and tilled for a use of farming for a harvest has a being and end, from the time the land is cleared, a seed ingrained into the soil until the harvest is celebrated, a begin and end of a harvest season. These are examples of use of a view of a door for rice, fruits and vegetables that I need everyday. Such views to doors have a time length for a view of a door such as a harvest for a begin and an end, a life of a seed to a plant for a begin and an end.

A view of door of a life of a human for a begin and an end can be related and written as a biography, a door of several views, viewed from the personal perspective(s) of a person that experienced the life for a begin and end of a life.

A view for a no fault - chapter 4

A compassion for an attitude!

A view of a door for not to fault any must be shown only as a progress for a path, a mistake I that I need to set right. I need to check the progress of the path for a curve of an ivy tree, a tree that grows horizontally, vertically or as a straight path showing several inches tall for a growth of a period, for a progress measured. A hindrance or an obstruction to the growth must be trimmed and the path set right for growth measured.

A view of a door for a no fault made is a mistake that must be evaluated and a solution found through a path of education and culture to help progress one for values of a family and work life, and must include diversity of values for a positive influence on society to generate a value positive.

A view for a no fault or a blame in society must be critiqued for a value of a positive result. A fault or blame attitude of someone in a family or society must be met using a quality of compassion that includes coaching and mentorship through guidance and counseling for a period of time aligned through a path of education and conversation, books, instruction for positive guidelines to make a favorable impact on every. A family that looks down negatively must be complemented with incentives for education, work and other incentives, that will have a positive impact on the family and others to generate a value positive for a value impact in society.

A value of a door for a no fault at a work place must be assessed by one for values that one has and values that they need for a balance of a positive impact on others. A view of a door I need to replace for a work ethic for a no fault must include good ethics practice for enforcement of a value, or values, delivery of work appreciated by the supervisor for every milestone met and other values. A failure in delivery of work must be assessed and balanced with training and mentorship from an organization for a positive impact of an employee for a no fault or blame. Such views to a door for no fault must be replaced with attributes of good conduct and ethics as a recognized employee of an organization.

A value for a no fault or a blame met in a real time environment includes examples of scenarios such as payments made by someone towards purchase of something not acknowledged by the customer service representative. Such a view to a door must be reviewed through problem resolution and a value of customer appreciation for a door of no fault met must be acknowledged. A purchase made not of quality must be accepted by the customer service rep for a no fault blame met.

A value of no fault for cultural intolerance must be communicated and translated to a training for inclusion of diversity of values for a balance of a conversation for a grace, tone, content to generate peace and harmony on both sides. The values of 5 for a relationship to progress must be enforced within and outside the home for a value of a no fault blame in all areas. The values of a no fault blame include, education for a grace of a conversation, a hospitality for an invitation and a fulfillment of a grace, a tone of voice for a renewal, peace for a silence of respect and a conversation appreciated by others for a harmony of an environment to continue the values enforced for a renewal.

A view for a no fault or a blame must be critiqued for a value of a positive result.

A fault or blame attitude of someone in a family or society must be met using a quality of compassion that includes coaching and mentorship through guidance and counseling for a period of time aligned through a path of education and conversation, books, instruction for positive guidelines to make a favorable impact on every. A family that looks down negatively must be complemented with incentives for education, work and other incentives, that will have a positive impact on the family and others to generate a value positive for a value impact in society.

A value of a door for a no fault at a work place must be assessed by one for values that one has and values that they need for a balance of a positive impact on others. A view of a door I need to replace for a work ethic for a no fault must include good ethics practice for enforcement of a value, or values, delivery of work appreciated by the supervisor for every milestone met and other values. A failure in delivery of work must be assessed and balanced with training and mentorship from an organization for a positive impact of an employee for a no fault or blame. Such views to a door for no fault must be replaced with attributes of good conduct and ethics as a recognized employee of an organization.

A value for a no fault or a blame met in a real time environment includes examples of scenarios such as payments made by someone towards purchase of something not acknowledged by the customer service representative. Such a view to a door must be reviewed through problem resolution and a value of customer appreciation for a door of no fault met must be acknowledged. A purchase made not of quality must be accepted by the customer service rep for a no fault blame met.

A value of no fault for cultural intolerance must be communicated and translated to a training for inclusion of diversity of values for a balance of a conversation for a grace, tone, content to generate peace and harmony on both sides. The values of 5 for a relationship to progress must be enforced within and outside the home for a value of a no fault blame in all areas. The values of a no fault blame include, education for a grace of a conversation, a hospitality for an invitation and a fulfillment of a grace, a tone of voice for a renewal, peace for a silence of respect and a conversation appreciated by others for a harmony of an environment to continue the values enforced for a renewal.

A view of a door I need to see for a best - chapter 5

A reason for a value best

A view of a door I need to see for a day and think the best must include

What I need to do to create a positive feeling and impact in my mind for a day and every day of my life. A day for when I wake up and learn that I have a terminal disease, only means that I need to exude a positive outlook and feeling for everyday and a lifetime not to be excluded by others. I need to create a picture in my mind that this disease can be cured if I take the right diet and obey the doctors for the treatment plan. I need to live in the present and only do activities that help me and others around me. I need to talk to people that would exude cheer and happiness and a positive impact when I hear them say something positive about me.

A view of a door for an improvement in relationship is a critique of an analysis for a result that will serve as a positive influence on others. This can include relationships for improvement of a family to go in the right path for activities that will make for a happy relationship. Such views to a door for a best include examples for a positive path such as offering food that they enjoy, watching movies or documentaries that are good for a family, interacting with people that will help understand the different situations for a problem solution.

A view of a door for a best for silence must include situations that help an emotion, a blame, a sadness, sorrow or others to help a situation or a relationship for an improvement. A silence will exude a positive feeling and positive health and create a positive impact on others. A silence unspoken is an image or a personality view that a person carries with him or her for a lifetime for a positive impression on others. A silence can be a positive impact for a gain or a bargain unspoken in family and work life. An action spoken is not a respect of silence for a positive impact unless a question asked for an answer

A view to a door of an appearance for the best for a positive attitude and impact will serve as a comparison critique for several situations and its evaluation a disquisition result for a positive or a negative influence and impact on any. A dress I wear in a setting is a value and exudes attributes such as if it covers me well from head to toe and will help in situations both positive and negative. I walk through a road where people take note of my appearance, I work in an environment where people look at my dress to evaluate my ethics for code of conduct and behavior. I dress for my family for a decency of value, I dress for a party for every question and stare. An appearance of a dress covering a body will exude a positive feeling for an assent in every setting. A view to a door for an appearance will be evaluated for points to synonym met for a dress code such as, has it covered my chest area, has it covered me fully for protection, has it covered my arms and feet, do I have my hair tied in a bun or a pony tail or a braid, and does my face have some makeup. If all points to a synonym are met for dress code rule, the points to synonym rule has been met.

A view of an action for an exchange must include kindness in talk, grace in hospitality, a conversation that exudes positivity for a praise of another for a well being, a hospitality for a food offered that exudes happiness in others. Such views to a door of best are examples of the following such as, A friend I invite to a meal with a grace, a friend I offer a food that she likes, A friend I converse on the well being of everyone, A friend I offer praise for an activity that created a positive result for an action and a feedback for the best.

A view, an apocryphal that I do not have an answer for, must not be pursued if there is no purpose or use. Such a view may be reviewed for a detail through literature support. An authority such as an educational institution may have an answer for such a view

A view for a conversation chapter 6

An approach for a new and renewal of friendship

A view of a conversation can be for a purpose and a benefit of one or for all in a group or others. A Conversation analysis (CA) is an approach to social research that investigates the sequential

Organization of talk as a way of accessing participants' understandings of, and collaborative means of organising, natural forms of social interaction (Hutchby, 2019)

The conversation can be and relate to an opinion of a few or others for the benefit of a few or others in a society.The conversation can be dominated by one or a few to make others feel low for a conversation theme that does not lend to respect or grace for renewal of friendships for harmony, grace, and appreciation of any.

A view to a door for a conversation can take the form of carelessness for a talk that does not bring value to any side, but that results in gossip or loss of values with or without truth and has no content except for a plea. This type of view to a door can take the form of jealousy, greed or dislike that they did not or could not attain what others did or they did not work towards a goal for a fulfillment or attainment.

A view of a conversation can include a view of a few for a superiority of their attitude over another of a person or group. This can take the form of a view to isolate a person or persons for the benefit of a person or a group. Such a view to a door for conversation must be eliminated and removed for a future recurrence by leaving the group and enrolling in a different group that includes diversity of values for family support and others.

A view to a door of a conversation of a person can also be for a disrespect of another person or persons only because of a prejudice of a person not to like a person for something or an attitude of a community of a person they think that others did not or do not have. A disrespect can take several forms of speech or acts if the person is not respected by a group of people.

A view to a door for a conversation can take the form for not to help another as a default and may include examples such as not to allow another into a circle of friendship for a reason not to help. A view of a conversation for not to like another can also include several examples of negative acts such as gesture of a hand or hands, a look in the eyes that shows dislike when conversing,

A scream or a rage, a walk fast, a restlessness only to think and hurt another, or enlisting the help of others in one or several communities to cause something to happen for a person not to be liked by a community or communities.

A view to a door for a conversation must include social norms for decency such as grace, appreciation, peace and harmony for all and by all.

A view at a glance - chapter 7

A collection of notes over time

A view at a glance to encompass everything includes a view outside and a view inside. A view outside, can be a conversation, a sport, a celebration, a difference of different cultures for a kindness and grace, a conversation for time, a season, or a setting for a context.

An inside view of a door for a view at a glance from a mind consists of an emotion, an embarrassment of words spoken, a disgrace of a behavior of another, a grace of a tone, a behavior of someone, a dress for a setting, and others for a measure of view at a glance for an impact both positive and negative.

An outside view of a glance can be an eye for an appreciation of something such as nature, seasons and others but a view of an assessment of a human personality leans between a negative and positive score for a measure of an attribute value. Such views of a door at a glance for a positive or negative outcome of a result is dependent on the help and support extended to another at a point of time.

A view of a person's mind and a view from once eyes is a difference of a view that can be positive or negative unless the interaction is through an experience first hand or is narrated positively. The view at a glance can also be positive If the person is someone precious to me, or of a culture or is related to me that I appreciate.

A view at a glance of a shopping experience I enjoy and a view at a glance of an exam I need to take is a difference of a stress, a negative feeling and a relaxation of a mind, a positive feeling that must be evaluated carefully, one for a success to a path of education and another for a purchase of an item and is an outing experience with my family.

A view at a glance can also be misinterpreted unless a view for a repeat of the same occurs and an evaluation must change for either a negative or a positive impact based on an outcome. An extreme opinion of a view to a door at a glance must be balanced using a judgement of peace and harmony factor, to revert an opinion of a such a view of a door to a reasonable judgement.

A view at a glance, a sharp criticism of another cannot be resolved unless the person goes through training and mentorship for a behavioral change. Such views to a door at a glance of criticism can occur either at home or at work and can have a negative impact on another causing disruption in one's life, interruption in one's thoughts of peace and harmony, not allowing one to show grace and appreciation in tone and manners and causing a negative impact on education, work and family life.

A View of a Trust for a Result -Chapter 8

A trust a value for a premise of life

A view of door to a trust, is several encounters of a person with another or a group and the result(s) an action for a renewal of friendship or a new friendship extending to a family relationship.

A trust is a value measured through a promise to deliver for an expectation based on a conversation or an agreement.

Examples include, A friend I agree to make some recipe for a party or a help I extend to someone in time of need, an agreement at work, a commitment to deliver on a contract for fulfillment.

A view of a door for a trust can also be viewed as an example of a person dependent on several factors such as if a person is related to another person, or if a person is an employee of an organization in a voluntary or involuntary capacity for fulfillment of a task. All or any of the above and others for such a view of a door of trust can be fulfilled either verbally or through a written agreement for a trust to build and extend for a view of a door of trust for a positive outcome and result in team support, team collaboration and team leadership.

A view of a door to a trust can benefit a person if the person maintains silence as a value of respect to support the value of friendship in any environment not to devalue the trust of another. Such views of door to a trust for a cause such as a failure to deliver a result, a positive compliment to build a trust will result in positive outcome for a view of a door of trust. Sometimes, views of door for trust may cause a negative impact for an outcome, but will ultimately translate to a relationship of trust resulting in a friendship, and also a mentorship for guidance and counseling resulting in a positive outcome, through continuous interactions to build a trust for delivery.

A view of a door for a trust is evaluated after a test of a person for a result of one or more actions and a path for a view of a door to a trust saved for future observations to build trust. A view of a door to a trust can also include causes for trust such as a trust for a care of young or older people. Such views of a door to a trust can be explained for causes such as a trust that I can entrust a person without a negative outcome or a trust not resulting in abuse or hostility.

A View to a door of a Family - Chapter 9

A value of a family, a lifetime

A door to a view of a family is an experience positive for each and every interaction for a life time. A door to a view of a family I was born into and a life I lived together with my parents and siblings In my home for a path of progress, a life of respect, an obedience in words and actions for sincerity, devotion, loyalty and trust for fulfillment of any a virtue is an embodiment of values such as help, and support through positive words and behavior to encourage positive initiatives as a friend for a lifetime.

A view to a door of a family is a support of a life time for commitment and fulfillment of all values for peace and harmony.

A view to a door of my family is a view of a door of positive outcomes for a lifetime. A view to a door of a family is a support of one at all times and in all phases of life such as a phase of a childhood, youth, middle age and old. Family members support each other a lifetime and at all times for better or worse.

Examples of a view to a door of a family include, a support I can trust and count on, words I cherish and respect, every an interaction only for a happiness of a life of laughter, a comfort of words, kindness of help extended at all times, and others.

A view of a family as a relation is a view I share for a happiness of one at all times such as for celebration of marriages, death, birth or for all others. This view can take the form of conversations that are pleasant, or otherwise but must embody support, trust and other virtues for a view of a door of a family. A view to a door of trust for a continuity of relationships, a lifetime is a view of a door of family relationships, a value of a lifetime.

A view to a door of a friend in some instances can also take the form of a family relationship from an outcome of help and support received as a friend or a mentor for a period of time.

A view to a door of several incident(s) that aggregate for a conclusion - chapter 10

A conclusion positive through an aggregation

A view of several interactions or conversations in any setting is evaluated as a view to a door of interactions that are renewed for new conversations or interactions and include values for a value of virtue for a pleasant, cheerful attitude, and include virtues to belong to an educated class for a skill set and expertise for a value to enhance.

A view to a door of aggregation for several interactions and conversations include positive outcome for a result meaningful between cultures. These conversations may be for a benefit of a mind and these benefits may include scenarios to be regarded as a member to attend coaching camps for a skill or a course, a friendship class for a learning of an art, a conversation class for a social event and others. Some of these interactions may include a fee for a learning of an education, a skill acquisition for knowledge for a use and others. Such views to doors of aggregation include a series of courses for a learning that will help build a brand for an art, and a communication skill for an expertise in a subject. These aggregations sum up the abstract summary the result of a conclusion and are shown as results for a grade through a certificate earned or a reward earned in cash or kind or an award received as a gift.

An interaction or events led by a group or a committee must be looked at by one as a series of courses created through a framework of rule(s) for a learning acquisition of a skill (knowledge for implementation) and must be followed by members of group for the benefit of every member for an outcome positive to lead others through a rule and case based scenario approach for a value of learning of a course.

A view to a door of several incidents must be reviewed for a value of a use for a purpose positive and must be discontinued for no value or no purpose.

These incidents must be measured and weighed for a benefit through a score for a measure of continuity for an education for a skill. A friendship of a learning is only for an occurrence of a learning of something such as education or a skill, and will promote friendship through peace and harmony for long-term relationships.

A view to a door, a disharmony a lifetime- chapter 11

A view of a disharmony everyday is only an impact negative for a mind of a lifetime. A disharmony may include a quarrel, an anger, a word that is inappropriate in a family setting, a work setting, a group setting, or others and will cause a disharmony for a lifetime. A disharmony will cause a life wasted of one by a group of people assembled against you unless a peace is mediated through an organization to set the disharmony to a state of peace and harmony using coaching and mentoring measures for peace and harmony in any setting.

A view of a disharmony must be eliminated and isolated for not to invite disharmony by any by moving towards an environment of peace and harmony for a lifetime. A value of disharmony must be translated using time as a measure for a harmony. A harmony must include values for adjustment for peace and harmony in any setting as long as it does not impact anyone negatively, such as a value of giving gifts to another to show harmony in a setting, a value of giving something in kind such as words of comfort or laughter for a harmony. Other values of harmony include values for encouraging book reading, book clubs for discussion to lead a class, watching educational channels for intelligence conversations for a respect of others for peace and harmony.

A disharmony in an environment is viewed for a loss of dignity, money, a profile wrongly painted of someone for destruction, an obstruction to the path of progress of one in the areas of education, work, and others. Such views to doors must be resolved through mediation of a family member, a counselor or others for solutions.

A disharmony also includes translating a profile, gentle and soft to a profile painted as a bad guy by others to take on the role of a destructor for the benefit of their own. This can take the form of a cruel or a bad person or a group that will cause a person to say words or act in a manner unjust, unfair, and criminal. These forces must be eliminated or removed from such a person or persons citing elements of disharmony harboring crime for an offense and dictated to by them for a cause of destruction either within a family or outside.

A disharmony also includes disturbance of a peace of mind of another by passing messages that are obscene, harmful, insensitive, bad or cruel that impact a human mind negatively for a lifetime. A disharmony can include elements of culture and culture sets of people that are taught at home or other settings to say words or cause behavior to be negative to people or groups that they do not like to result in a deterioration or a devaluation of another for not to progress in any area only because they do not like them for a reason in their mind. Such views to a door for a disharmony must be understood and moved away to new doors of harmony in a new setting. Other solutions include communicating with family members for a concrete solution not for a recurrence.

A view to a door of my thoughts for a difference of an impact - chapter 12

A view of thoughts to experience emotions such as for smile, wave, anger, sorrow, anxiety or others is a difference for a view to a door of an outcome either positive or negative. These emotions can make one's thoughts negative or positive based on the direction of thoughts for a path to success, or can translate memories of life's experiences to a path positive or negative.

A view to a door of a mind negative for a difference of a sorrow, sadness or negative attitude is a view that I should not carry with me for a long period of time. Such a view to a door for a difference must be reviewed and a new view replaced using either pictures in a book, a comedy show, prayers of peace, meditation for a relaxation, or a friendship positive for a conversation on varied topics such as food, movies or social norms for a positive relation to the world.

A view to a door of a mind for physical health not well must be understood through a view to a door for a difference through a balance of a diet of nutrition and exercise such as milk, yogurt, fruits, and vegetables etc. A balance for a health must include a class for extra curricular activities that will help the mind and body relax for activities such as for dance lessons, music lessons and others. A difference to a door of such a view must be measured for progress through a voice for happiness, a dance that I like and respect, a new knowledge I learnt and use every day.

A view to a door for a difference of a mind is an impact positive or negative on a mind and includes several views to a door of thoughts such as for a value of a profile or a personality of several for an impact. A profile or a personality for a difference of a value must include words that are appreciative and graceful, a charisma displayed through a coaching expertise in a subject area, a skill or an art translated into a course for a career, assembling of concepts of constructs learnt and translated into a syllabus for study in a subject area.

A view to a door of thoughts for a difference must also include skills to maintain and arrange something clean for a respect. A garden maintained well using an art, a home maintained well for a fragrance clean, an art or decor arranged for a grace, an appreciation of a virtue, or a respect for people for values of a difference for an impact positive.

A view to a door I need to watch - chapter 13

A view to a door for a watch is a door I need to watch for a purpose of safety of all, a family and others through peace and harmony. I need to watch words I communicate with another, I need to dress for a decency of a code of respect, I need to look and talk with respect to others for each and every an interaction, I need to keep track of my expenses, I need to bring a value across appreciated by others for an interaction. These are examples of a door I need to watch for myself for a door I need to maintain for a respect and appreciation at all times.

A door I need to watch for a difference positive for a safety must be selective and opened occasionally only for a knowledge acquisition, a progress in education or a promotion in a work area, a celebration event or others for an outcome positive, lest a door is opened for a threat and the door is not a viewed as a door of safety.

Other values to a door of watch for safety include values for commitment to deliver in a daily life such as a marriage for success in a family setting, responsibility for fulfillment of a role in family and work areas, friendly interactions with others for a safety of one and family

A door to watch for a value of safety must be seen as a door for fulfillment of values based on value goals of life of a family and others. These value goals must be measured every week for a value of progress every quarter and new goals measured and added for fulfillment of a value met of an individual in a family, work area, and others.

A View to a Door, A View Temporary - Chapter 14

A door temporary is a reason for a value of a door of continuity.

A view to a door temporary is a door that I view and stay at for education in a school, university and other educational areas, for a short time, or is an interaction at work for a few years, or is a social interaction with a few and others for a purpose. A view to a door for a door temporary must be renewed to a view of a door permanent through fulfillment of values for success in education, work or other areas through scores measured in areas such as increase in productivity of a work, contribution for a work performance exceeded, a value of a member I need for a lifetime, a new member and a friend, a family now, through a path of peace and harmony,

A view to a door temporary is a view of a door, a presence of someone for a short time, a lapse for an illness, a marriage temporary, a work temporary and others. The views to such doors is overcome over a period of time and is remembered every year for a reason of an anniversary or others for a loss of a presence or a job loss through training for an existing or new skill set for a job loss.

A view to a door temporary is a view of a door open for a peaceful purpose, a celebration of a season such as a festival, a gathering of families and friends for an event for birthday celebrations, and others. This view to a door is a door remembered often for memories of happiness cherished and made into stories of a book of happy memories of a family for recollection during festival times and others.

A view to a door temporary is a view to a door for a purpose of gathering for a short period of time for organizational goals, values group values for a value of virtue or organizational goals and strategies translated for fulfillment of business goals. These interactions are used for contribution of ideas and strategies of individuals for fulfillment of roles and responsibilities in a business or organizational setting.

A view to a door temporary is also for a discussion of role fulfillment for a role of responsibility at education, work and other areas. Such views to doors of education are positive for skills expertise, education, knowledge translation of work to productivity and others.

Sincerely,
Durga Madiraju

A view through a door and window a difference - chapter 15

A view to a door for a difference of a view of a window includes a disparate picture of a wide and large range of examples for a difference using a similarity or a comparison perspective. A view to a door through a window provides a sub-grouping of a whole, and is a subtraction of a view to a door through a description of characteristics of a physical view. The two can look similar except for a difference of a size. Such views to a door and window can be defined using a broader criteria for a similarity of a view and other criteria such as a view of a door or window for a season, a window for a safety, window for a view of a request and response, and others. An abstraction of a view of a door and a window for a definition must be used as a best definition for a meaning and difference of the two.

An archetypal view of a window is a narrow view of a door and can either be extended or reduced to stay within the boundary of a door or a window based on a use, reuse or a reason such as a need to see a view.

A view to a door I need to extend for a door to open is the door I need to include for a definition of a wide variety of topics for a door of knowledge to be shared. Several definitions of views to a door and window include relating a view of a door of a book to a story or stories I relate as a view of a new story to a door and a window.

Do these views match an experience I live every day? Stories that are positive must be used as examples and related for a positive outcome for a need of a daily or occasional use. Some examples of views to doors and windows for a difference of a whole and a subset, include using a recipe to make a dish, adding a dessert as a side, buying a model of clothing or jewelry for a saree match, watching an episode of a show and others.

A life's experience of a window and a door must be translated to a positive outcome.
A summer blue sky, I need to wear pastel shades. Clouds, a cool day, I need to make
A warm soup.

An impact negative at school or at work negative must be translated to an outcome positive for a learning of existing and new knowledge of sharing in all areas of life appreciated and respected.

An outside view of a door and a window may be too wide a topic for a relation of a view to a topic unless broken down by constructs for topics and subtopics and related through several subjects.

Several definitions of views to doors and windows must be aggregated and supported through literature using examples for definition and support of the term. An accretion of a view is to add new views or enhance existing views for a purpose or a need of a view in different areas of a subject for use at different levels and settings in different environments.

A circumlocution of a view to a door includes something that caught my eye such as stars in the sky, a rainbow, a rose, meadows or others and must be compared to an art such as a painting that I created, a graduation ceremony I worked hard for a degree, a celebration of a festival or a marriage for memories I cherish a life time. A definition of such a view must be used as a comparison, or a disquisition, or a critique of a topic for review and knowledge gathering.

A view for a difference of aberration must be eliminated for a replacement of a value positive. Such a view to a door and window must not be used to go down the path back for a use unless required. A view to a door that is abstruse must be broken down for simplicity of use and defined in relation to harmony of every.

A view of a door and window of history must not be used as an anachronistic view, if a review of the view causes a wrong relation or association for a discussion of a historical purpose. Some examples of views to doors and windows of history include use of new terms that need to be noted down by date and author for a reference to cite a source.

A view through a door for a whole - chapter 16

A view of a door for a whole includes all doors such as a door, a window and any. These views include a biased and unbiased opinion of a whole and must be translated well for an exposure or a display of someone or something to an outside world. The door for a whole must be restricted by parents for a view only for a decent, praiseworthy meetings such as a graceful view for a content, a graceful communication, a meeting for a purpose, a pleasant appearance and others.

A view of a door for a whole must include words that are required for communication to a world outside. These words must be defined in a family dictionary and associated with a sentence that must be ingrained for use by a family such as a welcome greeting, a conversation for the meeting, a and a graceful exit of a guest.

A view of a door for a whole must include education that can be seen with respect in the eyes of family and others for a value of an education correct and needed for a job

For a path of progress and promotion. A job I work at must include intelligence of a skill of a work for use and reuse in an organization. A skill that earns the respect of a well learnt person for an education of sophistication embodied in the job skill and delivery.

A view of a door for a whole for a presentation to an outside world must be entwined as a twig and include a flower and leaf in a bark, a flower and a bow, a bud, flower and leaf, a customized sophistication, an embodiment of all values earned of skills to assemble a custom skill to earn a work, and others.

A view of a door for a whole of a receptiveness must include values such as a grace, a decor, a decorum, a comfort to a receive or a send, a welcome of a hospitality offered and received, and others. A mother that embodies all the values for affection, grace, comfort, and is there for a need of the family earns the respect and affection of everyone in the family.

A view of a door for a whole must include words that are positive only and must carry a person with enthusiasm and sophistication for an entire day and night and for a life time of rich values

These words must serve as a renewal to invite existing and new friendships for for a lifetime.

A view to a door, A Friendly Approach - chapter 17

A view to a door for a friendly approach is a view of a door I interact with on a daily or occasional basis with a cheerful and pleasant attitude. A greeting and an acknowledgement, a conversation using a friendly approach of inquiring about the well being of a family, a few outlines about general home questions and others. Such a view to a door of a friendly approach interactions must receive positive note for communication and feedback, a receptive tone for an interaction and others. Such views to a door of a friendly approach must use a tone and an expression gentle and graceful for a view I need to respect at all times.

This view to a door for a friendly approach must be kept open at all times, a door that I can enter with confidence, comfort, support and appreciation Such views to a door initiate an approach of friendship for progress and growth of a family, a view to a door kept open for good and bad times, and any day of a season.

A door to a friendly approach can be used to gather knowledge for a number of uses and seasons.

There are other doors and avenues also one must look at for values of friendship for a path of progress and growth. A door of friendship must be viewed as a peaceful and a happy interaction for a continuity of friendship a lifetime translating into a role for a job as a volunteer, or as a valued employee and others.

A door to a friendly approach must always use new knowledge approaches for a view to a door of peace and harmony for reasons such as peaceful co-existence. Such views to a door for a friendly approach must align to new initiatives for harmony using examples and scenarios for interactions in a community such as celebration of an occasion, a support for a help of illness of another, a contribution for the growth of community for a benefit of every member of the community.

A view to a door of a friendly approach must always be remembered for new uses and purposes. A door friendly or the view of other doors friendly towards this door must be used for creating new values in the community using a door of comfort, support and appreciation for positive outcomes through coaching, mentoring, knowledge interaction and others to add value to the community.

A view to a door- A View I Build - Chapter 18

A view to a door I build is a door of views I gathered over a period of time, a season of all seasons to understand and relate a door for a difference of a culture, a custom, tradition and others for a celebration, an educational progress, a career growth and others to build new views to a door of art, book, culture and others

The door to a view I build can include aspects of life that impact a mind for emotions of an experience, such as a door of values for a food habit, a cooking recipe, a culture for an interaction to bring new doors of friendship into a family, an acknowledgement of a milestone and others.

A comprehensive view of a door can also be used to write a note or a disquisition for an enrichment of a value(s) in ones life such as a reminder for a continuity of positive values for progress and growth, a lifetime. Such views to doors can be built for teaching, coaching or for other purposes for positive behavioral values such as for manners, respect, appreciation, conversation, cooking and others.

A view to a door I build seasons over a period may also include doors of books that I read and capture in mind and write with new values. A book of a herb is a grace I need for all seasons, for to eat and stay healthy a lifetime. A book of an ivy plant is a book I need to know the temperature of for the water content and the type of pot for the growth of an ivy all seasons. These books help us to create new pictures with new content for new books such as, A season, an ivy, a difference. A herb new, for a fragrance and a friendship to grow.

A view to a door, A door for best - chapter 19

A view to a door for a door for best is a door, I am amenable to, to understand and provide a solution for amenability from a door of hostility to a door of peace, from a door of devaluation to a door of appreciation, from a door of poor grace to door of grace and manners. Such views to doors are exuded through education, books, social interaction and others. A view to a door that provides mentorship and coaching is a door that sets a guideline of principles of value of virtues for progress and growth. Such views to doors must be adhered to within a community to exude harmony, a daily necessity, respect, a support of peaceful coexistence and silence, a knowledge of interactions between people.

A view to a door for the best is a door I look up to in an organization, a community, a counselor, or a family with the highest education such as a doctorate for knowledge sharing and enactment of positive values through mentorship, grace, a tone for a conversation, and a value of knowledge received and translated for a value of a problem to a solution.

A view to a door of the best is a view of a door of seasons, a value that I can relate to for a best, a summer view of a door, an autumn view of a door, a winter, a new view of a door. Such views of doors are value views that I need to learn for the best view of a door of season to exude values of grace, tone, manners and knowledge that I exude for a value of knowledge exhibited through education or work, for every question answered in a setting.

A view for a door closed - chapter 20

A view to a door of a view closed can be of thoughts confined to a mind within, or a door shut at home, a mind or an association for a knowledge not to extend or share.

A door closed can be for a reason of a view of a mind to divert a mind for a view to pursue education for a progress of knowledge, a view of a door that shows several people highly educated with skill sets and expertise in different subjects. Such a view of a door is a knowledge I associate through my education and extend this education for progress and growth to benefit several areas of life such as family, work, community, organization, and others.

A view of a door closed can be for a view of a door closed for a reason of death of someone that I associated with, a spouse, a parent, a friend or others, and is only remembered through memories for a day or two in a year, and these memories fade for time and replaced with new memories. Such views of a door to a trust are views of doors closed for new doors to open for new confidence to a role as a leader in every and all areas subject through knowledge acquisition, skill set, training and exercise simulation for experience.

A view of a door closed of a mind can be reopened with new thoughts of new people, new friends, new relationships from marriage, education, work and others that make a positive impact in their mind and life for a lifetime.

A view of a door closed can also be for a view of a new door opened of respect for collaboration and participation that I acquired from educating myself, and several doors of respect and value that opened within my own home and outside,

Such views of doors opened new friendships, new work and new trust relationships in several areas for sharing of new knowledge. Such views of doors also result in new family relationships such as a marriage to a friend, a new subject I created that created several subjects, a new art learnt, a new skill that translated to mentorship and coaching of others.

An abstraction for a view of a new door is opened for research using literature for review, critique or disquisition for new notes and new knowledge studies. Such views of doors are reviewed for feedback for comments and new knowledge added for a complete literature of a new subject.

A view of a door closed opens several avenues of new doors for creativity using a mind for research from several topics online or creating constructs from vocabulary for extension and addition to new knowledge studies.

A view to a door challenged - Chapter 21

A value translation for an amenable character

A view to a door challenged is a door I need to translate for virtues and values of grace, peace, harmony, trust, support and others. A support of a friend, a voice and tone is a virtue that will translate a hostile attitude of one for a positive outcome such as for an attitude of an amenable and peaceful profile.

An example of a door challenged is a view of a door to disrupt or disturb another with challenges to disturb a peace of mind from performing activities for education, work or others either at home, work or in other environments. Such views to doors for challenges can come from a lack of education, skill, training or others for a need to converse negatively to cause destruction of progress for growth. A value of love and support must be extended to remove challenges for such situations so that they are eliminated or removed for a lifetime.

The reasons for a view to a door of challenge must be questioned for a solution. Examples of such views of doors for a challenge include an acquisition of an asset by another through unfair means, a dislike of another for no reason except for a value of comparison from their point of view, a dislike of person that a skill match is not right just for reasons of complacency, a need for a challenge to cause irritation of another, a value of challenge ingrained as a virtue of one and not as a trait for removal. Such views of door to challenges must be removed and new values ingrained such as virtues for peace and harmony to include values for commitment and devotion for work, a support as a team member for participation and collaboration.

A view to a door of challenge is a door I need to be aware of to understand through diligence and perseverance the removal of a challenge(s) replaced with values of virtues for grace, social etiquette, consideration, appreciation, through enriched knowledge using effective content and communication.

The view to a door for such challenges can be removed by a highly educated person such as a Professor who can translate these values to virtues for a role of a mentor, coach, counselor and others through effective communication using a collaborative support framework of peace and harmony.

A view to a door
Negative - chapter 22

A virtue and a reason for a positive influence, and an impact

A view to a door negative is a door I do not wish to see for an outcome negative. A positive influence for an attitude of a door positive is a door that people look at with respect for their own peace of mind.

A negative value such as a feeling for a negativity, a hostile attitude, a dislike displayed by others, is a view of a door watched with hostility and negative attitude of other doors and this door is a door viewed by others as a view of a door of a poor performer with negative attitude in areas such as education, skills, work and family values.

A negative attitude of a view of a door will prevent a family or others from going out and talking to others about such doors for fear that they can be viewed as having a negative influence and impact on others. A view to a door negative is a door where someone only tries to aggregate faults or words of another door for a complaint to the extent of sending messages through emails and other social media to create a negative profile or negative value of another in the community in personal, work or other areas.

A view to a door negative must be prevented or eliminated immediately through talking to family and support organizations that help them and others for help in removing the negative influences of negative impact of others on a door.

The view to a door negative is very prevalent of a society driven through a culture set of values and habits, a narrow view and outlook of a view of a door, that should and should not, a restriction rule, a forbidden rule learnt from their scriptures, created by themselves or their cultural values and that other cultures are not aware of. These values must be separated for a peaceful and positive harmony of a door, for a door of negativity not to cause an impact or influence another door.

A community or an organization must review all rules of door to adhere to laws of peace and harmony for existence of a human being not to encroach, cause a disruption, not to disturb, not to cause damage and others and must coexist peacefully using principles of panchsheel for peaceful coexistence in any setting.

A view to a door for a trust - Chapter 23

A view of a door inside my home is a door I trust for the length of time I stayed and respected at all times. A view of a door I was born into and raised by my parents, a view of a life I lived with my parents and siblings until I graduated and left for a new view of a door of marriage or work.

A view of a door I trust is a view of a door of my home for the trust and support I earned through peace and harmony created either alone, or through my marriage, and through growth of my family.

A view of a door I trust of my work is a view of the door I trust for the length of my employment at work, my work performance, the company that trusted me, and embodied for values of devotion, sincerity and loyalty for a progress of values of growth through education and learning at different levels.

A view of a door is a view of a door I trust, a trust earned through respect as a family member, as a friend, in an education, work or at the organizational setting level. This trust is a view of a door of a trust earned through dedication and sincerity towards my family for virtues of loyalty, obedience, sincerity and devotion towards my family and others.

A view to a door of trust is a view I see of my family. Years of a mother, dedicated and sincere to her children, cooking, buying things everyone likes, celebrating family birthdays and festivals and working with children coaching for education in different subjects, helping teach and relate values of virtues for a success of a path of progress, and solving problems encountered in different areas of life at every level of setting.

A trust is a eulogy and an award we see for continuity of a path to success at different levels of success in different areas of life meeting all requirements for progress and growth and making an impact positive in one's mind and on others. A trust extended for support is a voluntary service rendered in a community, a coaching given for a subject for a new skill learning, an advice rendered that helped someone and others.

A view to a door I need to understand for better - chapter 24

A view to a door, I need to understand of all disquisitions of a feedback, I collected at home, family, and outside is a review of the views collected and noted down as a list for use. These views must be aligned to a meaning and value for a view of a door I need to see for a need at different levels of setting such as at the family level, education level, work level and others. Such views of doors for virtues must be met through different points assigned to a synonym for a synonym met of a virtue of understanding of a view for a door of virtue.

The above views must be translated to solutions for a problem identified and met through a simulation in real world environment for a newer and higher level of learning in all areas to prevent existing or future recurrences of views to a door for an understanding of a view to a door.

A door to a family value of virtues must be set at very high levels and met through conversations for a tone, a silence for a learning, an obedience for a devotion and commitment for a delivery, a dress for an occasion for renewal of a virtue, and an exchange of information for a value of a learning for collaboration and trust.

A door to a work value must be identified through exercising of code of ethics for good conduct, for an arrival to work on time until the time of departure in a work setting. Values of work for delivery must include a work ethic for a work delivery met in all areas of work for a role fulfillment. All work values must be met through appreciation for work recognized and certified by the organization.

A door to a value as a member of a community for a harmony of a group must include values as a member of trust and support listed in community guidelines for contribution of values to the community for an appreciation and respect of every member for a view of a door I understand better.

A view to a door for a view correct - Chapter 25

A view to a door I need to view for a path of progress in any setting is a view I need to look at for peace and harmony. A view must be positive for a use or an outcome of a value met and does not have a negative impact on a task or a mind. Such a view is a view in every setting that I must look at positively and that meets all qualities of a view to a door of peace and harmony. A view to a door positive must be translated for an interaction and occurrence for a value met for peace and harmony.

A negative occurrence must be balanced through mentorship and coaching through skills acquisition that would help values progress for a balanced view of peace and harmony for all values met for fulfillment.

A negative occurrence must also be overcome through positive collaboration using an attitude of friendship as a contributor and a lead through expertise in problem resolution using a solution approach for a view of all doors of a correct view.

A view to a door for a view I need to see comes from a result of a learning, such as a grade in an exam from pursuing an education, a performance evaluation from performance at work, a periodic review of quality and quantity of work completed for a time period and others. Some examples of such views are, A work contribution that helped increase productivity to generate new work, a work activity that received a positive review for an outcome of a result. These examples of views to doors are a value path for continuity to a path of progress for a life of peace and harmony.

A view to a door for a view I need to see also comes from a view of one that receives a family coaching, an educational learning, a work learning and others for a path of progress to continue to a higher level of education and learning at work for a role of responsibility embarking on a path of fulfillment of work using peace and harmony as a strategy.

Part 2 - Jane Summers Programming Language

1. A match for something

Symbols Meaning is listed below:

Infinity = match
a infinity b - A match to complement a whole
Any complement!
A trouser and shirt!
A dress and shoes and a scarf

2. Points to synonym Met
£ = number of points
a=£<a:n>
Peace:
Met through prayers
Met through meditation as a relaxation
Met for a sleep
Met to read a book
Met to write something

3. Points for negative rules
a=<a-n>
Remove rules that are negative from the
Disquisition critiqued

4. A Disquisition(s)

a=<a:n>

An abstract summary or an essay

5. Compare critique method
a=<a:n-I>

A comparison of several articles reviewed
Yo arrive at a abstract disquisition

6. Ivy curve method
a=<a:&n + n>

Several ivy curves similar a growth + a growth of a leaf everyday until complete to attrition.

7. Pick Continuity Method:
$= pick

Pick for a continuity .. an aggregation
a=<a$a:n>
Pick a rule(s) for an aggregation of rules

8. Wastage Elimination Method
Wastage = ~
a=<a~<a-n>>

9. Utils for a point

#= utils assigned as a point
a#<a:n>

10. Core Value

A core value identified from a list of values
Core=@
a=<a@a:n>

[Extract is a function]

Extract()
(
Comments = [] for begin and end
[a=<a:n>]
Extract a dress
a=<a1=skirt:a2=blouse:a3=shoes>
a=dress [match using a complement]
)

Printed in the United States
by Baker & Taylor Publisher Services